MANCHESTER UNITED

MON		14	28
TUE	01	15	29
WED	02	16	30
THU	03	17	31
FRI	04	18	
SAT	05	19	
SUN	06	20	
MON	07	21	
TUE	08	22	
WED	09	23	
THU	10	24	
FRI	11	25	
SAT	12	26	
SUN	13	27	

JANUARY

- 01 - New Year's Holiday
  (UK & Republic of Ireland)
- 02 - Holiday (Scotland)

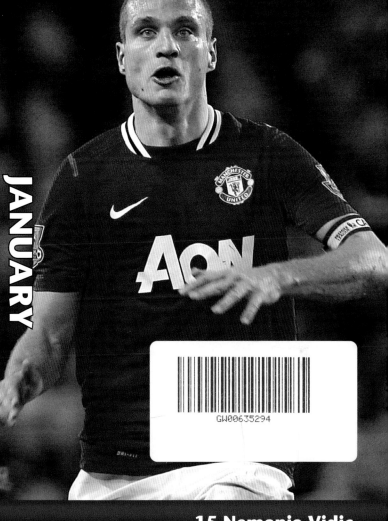

15 Nemanja Vidic

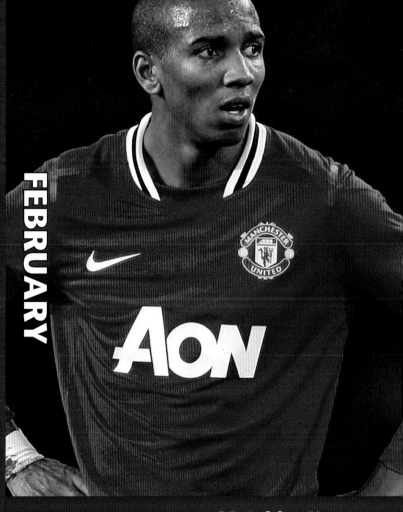

FEBRUARY

MON	11	25
TUE	12	26
WED	13	27
THU	14	28
FRI	01	15
SAT	02	16
SUN	03	17
MON	04	18
TUE	05	19
WED	06	20
THU	07	21
FRI	08	22
SAT	09	23
SUN	10	24

- 10 - Chinese New Year
- 13 - Ash Wednesday
- 14 - St. Valentine's Day

18 Ashley Young

MANCHESTER UNITED

MARCH

MON		11	25
TUE		12	26
WED		13	27
THU		14	28
FRI	01	15	29
SAT	02	16	30
SUN	03	17	31
MON	04	18	
TUE	05	19	
WED	06	20	
THU	07	21	
FRI	08	22	
SAT	09	23	
SUN	10	24	

- 01 - St. David's Day (Wales)
- 10 - Mothering Sunday (UK)
- 17 - St. Patrick's Day (Ireland)
- 18 - St. Patrick's Day Holiday (Ireland)
- 29 - Good Friday (UK)
- 31 - Easter Sunday
- 31 - Daylight Saving Begins

26 Shinji Kagawa

MON	01	15	29
TUE	02	16	30
WED	03	17	
THU	04	18	
FRI	05	19	
SAT	06	20	
SUN	07	21	
MON	08	22	
TUE	09	23	
WED	10	24	
THU	11	25	
FRI	12	26	
SAT	13	27	
SUN	14	28	

APRIL

10 Wayne Rooney

- 01 - Easter Monday
  (UK & Republic of Ireland)
- 23 - St. George's Day (England)

MANCHESTER UNITED

MAY

MON		13	27
TUE		14	28
WED	01	15	29
THU	02	16	30
FRI	03	17	31
SAT	04	18	
SUN	05	19	
MON	06	20	
TUE	07	21	
WED	08	22	
THU	09	23	
FRI	10	24	
SAT	11	25	
SUN	12	26	

• 06 - May Day Holiday
   (UK & Republic of Ireland)
• 27 - Spring Holiday (UK)

1 David De Gea

JUNE

MON		10	24
TUE		11	25
WED		12	26
THU		13	27
FRI		14	28
SAT	01	15	29
SUN	02	16	30
MON	03	17	
TUE	04	18	
WED	05	19	
THU	06	20	
FRI	07	21	
SAT	08	22	
SUN	09	23	

- 16 - Father's Day
- 21 - Longest Day

22 Paul Scholes

JULY

MON	01	15	29
TUE	02	16	30
WED	03	17	31
THU	04	18	
FRI	05	19	
SAT	06	20	
SUN	07	21	
MON	08	22	
TUE	09	23	
WED	10	24	
THU	11	25	
FRI	12	26	
SAT	13	27	
SUN	14	28	

• 12 - Holiday (Northern Ireland)

5 Rio Ferdinand

AUGUST

MON		12	26
TUE		13	27
WED		14	28
THU	01	15	29
FRI	02	16	30
SAT	03	17	31
SUN	04	18	
MON	05	19	
TUE	06	20	
WED	07	21	
THU	08	22	
FRI	09	23	
SAT	10	24	
SUN	11	25	

- 05 - Holiday
  (Scotland & Rep of Ireland)
- 26 - Late Summer Holiday (UK)

16 Michael Carrick

SEPTEMBER

MON	09	23
TUE	10	24
WED	11	25
THU	12	26
FRI	13	27
SAT	14	28
SUN	01	15	29
MON	02	16	30
TUE	03	17	
WED	04	18	
THU	05	19	
FRI	06	20	
SAT	07	21	
SUN	08	22	

- 05 - Rosh Hashanah
  (Jewish New Year)
- 14 - Yom Kippur
  (Day of Atonement)
- 21 - The United Nations
  International Day of Peace

7 Antonio Valencia

OCTOBER

MON		14	28
TUE	01	15	29
WED	02	16	30
THU	03	17	31
FRI	04	18	
SAT	05	19	
SUN	06	20	
MON	07	21	
TUE	08	22	
WED	09	23	
THU	10	24	
FRI	11	25	
SAT	12	26	
SUN	13	27	

- 27 - Daylight Saving Ends
- 28 - Holiday
  (Republic of Ireland)
- 31 - Halloween

4 Phil Jones

MANCHESTER UNITED

NOVEMBER

MON		11	25
TUE		12	26
WED		13	27
THU		14	28
FRI	01	15	29
SAT	02	16	30
SUN	03	17	
MON	04	18	
TUE	05	19	
WED	06	20	
THU	07	21	
FRI	08	22	
SAT	09	23	
SUN	10	24	

- 03 - Diwali
- 05 - Al Hijra
- 10 - Remembrance Sunday
- 30 - St. Andrews Day
  (Scotland)

19 Danny Welbeck

DECEMBER

MON		09	23
TUE		10	24
WED		11	25
THU		12	26
FRI		13	27
SAT		14	28
SUN	01	15	29
MON	02	16	30
TUE	03	17	31
WED	04	18	
THU	05	19	
FRI	06	20	
SAT	07	21	
SUN	08	22	

- 21 - Shortest Day
- 25 - Christmas Day
- 26 - Boxing Day
- 26 - St. Stephen's Day
  (Republic of Ireland)

17 Nani